KU-457-208

Confidentiality

This guidance comes into effect on 12 October 2009

plain English
appro√ed
by the word centre

General
Medical
Council

Regulating doctors
Ensuring good medical practice

Contents

About this guidance

1   Being registered with the General Medical Council gives you rights and privileges. In return, you have a duty to meet the standards of competence, care and conduct set by the GMC.

2   *Good Medical Practice* makes clear that patients have a right to expect that information about them will be held in confidence by their doctors. This guidance sets out the principles of confidentiality and respect for patients' privacy that you are expected to understand and follow.

3   You must use your judgement to apply the principles in this guidance to the situations you face in your own practice. The purpose of this guidance is to help you identify the relevant legal and ethical considerations, and to help you make decisions that respect patients' privacy, autonomy and choices, and that also benefit the wider community of patients and the public. If in doubt, you should seek the advice of experienced colleagues, a Caldicott Guardian[1] or equivalent, or your professional or regulatory body.

4   Supplementary guidance is available on our website explaining how these principles apply in situations doctors often encounter or find hard to deal with. We propose to review that supplementary guidance regularly to keep it up to date and relevant to the problems doctors face. At the time of publishing this core guidance, we are also publishing supplementary guidance on:

(a) reporting concerns about patients to the DVLA
(b) disclosing records for financial and administrative purposes
(c) reporting gunshot and knife wounds
(d) disclosing information about serious communicable diseases
(e) disclosing information for insurance, employment and similar purposes
(f) disclosing information for education and training purposes
(g) responding to criticism in the press.

5   Serious or persistent failure to follow this guidance will put your registration at risk.

Principles

6   Confidentiality is central to trust between doctors and patients. Without assurances about confidentiality, patients may be reluctant to seek medical attention or to give doctors the information they need in order to provide good care. But appropriate information sharing is essential to the efficient provision of safe, effective care, both for the individual patient and for the wider community of patients.

7   You should make sure that information is readily available to patients explaining that, unless they object, their personal information may be disclosed for the sake of their own care and for local clinical audit. Patients usually understand that information about them has to be shared within the healthcare team to provide their care. But it is not always clear to patients that others who support the provision of care might also need to have access to their personal information. And patients may not be aware of disclosures to others for purposes other than their care, such as service planning or medical research. You must inform patients about disclosures for purposes they would not reasonably expect, or check that they have already received information about such disclosures.

8   Confidentiality is an important duty, but it is not absolute. You can disclose personal information if:

   (a) it is required by law (see paragraphs 17 to 23)

   (b) the patient consents – either implicitly for the sake of their own care (see paragraphs 25 to 31) or expressly for other purposes (see paragraphs 32 to 35)

   (c) it is justified in the public interest (see paragraphs 36 to 56).

9   When disclosing information about a patient, you must:

(a) use anonymised or coded information if practicable and if it will serve the purpose

(b) be satisfied that the patient:

    (i) has ready access to information that explains that their personal information might be disclosed for the sake of their own care, or for local clinical audit, and that they can object, and

    (ii) has not objected

(c) get the patient's express consent if identifiable information is to be disclosed for purposes other than their care or local clinical audit, unless the disclosure is required by law or can be justified in the public interest

(d) keep disclosures to the minimum necessary, and

(e) keep up to date with, and observe, all relevant legal requirements, including the common law and data protection legislation.[2]

10   When you are satisfied that information should be disclosed, you should act promptly to disclose all relevant information.

11   You should respect, and help patients to exercise, their legal rights to:

(a) be informed about how their information will be used, and

(b) have access to, or copies of, their health records.[3]

Protecting information

12 You must make sure that any personal information about patients that you hold or control is effectively protected at all times against improper disclosure. The UK health departments publish guidance on how long health records should be kept and how they should be disposed of. You should follow the guidance whether or not you work in the NHS.[4]

13 Many improper disclosures are unintentional. You should not share identifiable information about patients where you can be overheard, for example, in a public place or in an internet chat forum. You should not share passwords or leave patients' records, either on paper or on screen, unattended or where they can be seen by other patients, unauthorised healthcare staff, or the public.

14 Unless they have a relevant management role, doctors are not expected to assess the security standards of large-scale computer systems provided for their use in the NHS or in other managed healthcare environments. You should familiarise yourself with and follow policies and procedures designed to protect patients' privacy where you work and when using computer systems provided for your use. This includes policies on the use of laptops and portable media storage devices. You must not abuse your access privileges and must limit your access to information you have a legitimate reason to view.

15 If you are responsible for the management of patient records or other patient information, you should make sure that they are held securely and that any staff you manage are trained and understand their responsibilities. You should make use of professional expertise when selecting and developing systems to record, access and send electronic data.[5] You should make sure that administrative information, such as names and addresses, can be accessed separately from clinical information so that sensitive information is not displayed automatically.

16 If you are concerned about the security of personal information in premises or systems provided for your use, you should follow the advice in *Good Medical Practice* on raising concerns about patient safety, including concerns about confidentiality and information governance.

Disclosures required by law

Disclosures required by statute

17 You must disclose information to satisfy a specific statutory requirement, such as notification of a known or suspected case of certain infectious diseases.[6]

18 Various regulatory bodies have statutory powers to access patients' records as part of their duties to investigate complaints, accidents or health professionals' fitness to practise. You should satisfy yourself that any disclosure sought is required by law or can be justified in the public interest. Many regulatory bodies have codes of practice governing how they will access and use personal information.

19 Whenever practicable, you should inform patients about such disclosures, unless that would undermine the purpose, even if their consent is not required.

20 Patient records or other personal information may be required by the GMC or other statutory regulators for an investigation into a healthcare professional's fitness to practise. If information is requested, but not required by law, or if you are referring concerns about a health professional to a regulatory body, you must, if practicable, seek the patient's express consent before disclosing personal information. If a patient refuses to consent, or if it is not practicable to seek their consent, you should contact the appropriate regulatory body, to help you decide whether the disclosure can be justified in the public interest.[7]

Disclosures to courts or in connection with litigation

21   You must disclose information if ordered to do so by a judge or presiding officer of a court. You should object to the judge or the presiding officer if attempts are made to compel you to disclose what appears to you to be irrelevant information, such as information about a patient's relative who is not involved in the proceedings.

22   You must not disclose personal information to a third party such as a solicitor,[8] police officer or officer of a court without the patient's express consent, unless it is required by law or can be justified in the public interest.

23   In Scotland, the system of precognition means there can be limited disclosure of information in advance of a criminal trial, to both the Crown and Defence, without the patient's express consent. The disclosure must be confined solely to the nature of injuries, the patient's mental state, or pre-existing conditions or health, documented by the examining doctor, and their likely causes. If they want further information, either side may apply to the court to take a precognition on oath. If that happens, you will be given advance warning and you should seek legal advice about what you can and cannot disclose.

Disclosing information with consent

24   Seeking a patient's consent to disclosure of information shows respect, and is part of good communication between doctors and patients.

Circumstances in which patients may give implied consent to disclosure

Sharing information within the healthcare team or with others providing care

25   Most patients understand and accept that information must be shared within the healthcare team in order to provide their care. You should make sure information is readily available to patients explaining that, unless they object, personal information about them will be shared within the healthcare team, including administrative and other staff[9] who support the provision of their care.

26   This information can be provided in leaflets, posters, on websites, and face to face and should be tailored to patients' identified needs as far as practicable. Posters might be of little assistance to patients with sight impairment or who do not read English, for example. In reviewing the information provided to patients, you should consider whether patients would be surprised to learn about how their personal information is being used and disclosed.

27   You must respect the wishes of any patient who objects to particular personal information being shared within the healthcare team or with others providing care, unless disclosure would be justified in the public interest. If a patient objects to a disclosure that you consider essential to the provision of safe care, you should explain that you cannot refer them or otherwise arrange for their treatment without also disclosing that information.

28   You must make sure that anyone you disclose personal information to understands that you are giving it to them in confidence, which they must respect. All staff members receiving personal information in order to provide or support care are bound by a legal duty of confidence, whether or not they have contractual or professional obligations to protect confidentiality.

29   Circumstances may arise in which a patient cannot be informed about the disclosure of information, for example, in a medical emergency. In such a case you should pass relevant information promptly to those providing the patient's care. If and when the patient is capable of understanding, you should inform them how their personal information was disclosed if it was in a way they would not reasonably expect.

Local clinical audit

30   All doctors in clinical practice have a duty to participate in clinical audit and to contribute to National Confidential Inquiries.[10] If an audit is to be undertaken by the team that provided care, or those working to support them, such as clinical audit staff, you may disclose identifiable information, provided you are satisfied that the patient:

(a) has ready access to information that explains that their personal information may be disclosed for local clinical audit, and that they have the right to object, and

(b) has not objected.

31   If a patient does object, you should explain why the information is needed and how this may benefit their own, and others' care. If it is not possible to provide safe care without disclosing information for audit, you should explain this to the patient and the options open to them.

32 If clinical audit is to be undertaken, but not by the team that provided care or those who support them, the information should be anonymised or coded. If this is not practicable, or if identifiable information is essential to the audit, you should disclose the information only if you have the patient's express consent. (See the guidance on *Research and other uses* in paragraphs 40 to 50.)

Disclosures for which express consent should be sought

33 As a general rule, you should seek a patient's express consent before disclosing identifiable information for purposes other than the provision of their care or local clinical audit, such as financial audit and insurance or benefits claims.[11]

34 If you are asked to provide information to third parties, such as a patient's insurer or employer or a government department or an agency assessing a claimant's entitlement to benefits, either following an examination or from existing records, you should:

(a) be satisfied that the patient has sufficient information about the scope, purpose and likely consequences of the examination and disclosure, and the fact that relevant information cannot be concealed or withheld

(b) obtain or have seen written consent to the disclosure from the patient or a person properly authorised to act on the patient's behalf; you may accept an assurance from an officer of a government department or agency or a registered health professional acting on their behalf that the patient or a person properly authorised to act on their behalf has consented

(c) only disclose factual information you can substantiate, presented in an unbiased manner, relevant to the request; so you should not usually disclose the whole record, although it may be relevant to some benefits paid by government departments and to other assessments of patients' entitlement to pensions or other health-related benefits, and

(d) offer to show your patient, or give them a copy of, any report you write about them for employment or insurance purposes before it is sent, unless:

(i) they have already indicated they do not wish to see it

(ii) disclosure would be likely to cause serious harm to the patient or anyone else

(iii) disclosure would be likely to reveal information about another person who does not consent.[12]

35 If a patient refuses consent, or if it is not practicable to get their consent, information can still be disclosed if it is required by law or can be justified in the public interest (see paragraphs 36 to 56). If the purpose is covered by a regulation made under section 251 of the *NHS Act 2006*, disclosures can also be made without a patient's consent, but not if the patient has objected.[13]

The public interest

Disclosures in the public interest

36 There is a clear public good in having a confidential medical service. The fact that people are encouraged to seek advice and treatment, including for communicable diseases, benefits society as a whole as well as the individual. Confidential medical care is recognised in law as being in the public interest. However, there can also be a public interest in disclosing information: to protect individuals or society from risks of serious harm, such as serious communicable diseases or serious crime; or to enable medical research, education or other secondary uses of information that will benefit society over time.

37 Personal information may, therefore, be disclosed in the public interest, without patients' consent, and in exceptional cases where patients have withheld consent, if the benefits to an individual or to society of the disclosure outweigh both the public and the patient's interest in keeping the information confidential. You must weigh the harms that are likely to arise from non-disclosure of information against the possible harm, both to the patient and to the overall trust between doctors and patients, arising from the release of that information.

38 Before considering whether a disclosure of personal information would be justified in the public interest, you must be satisfied that identifiable information is necessary for the purpose, or that it is not reasonably practicable to anonymise or code it. In such cases, you should still seek the patient's consent unless it is not practicable to do so, for example, because:

(a) the patient is not competent to give consent, in which case you should consult the patient's welfare attorney, court-appointed deputy, guardian or the patient's relatives, friends or carers (see paragraphs 57 to 63)

(b) you have reason to believe that seeking consent would put you or others at risk of serious harm

(c) seeking consent would be likely to undermine the purpose of the disclosure, for example, by prejudicing the prevention or detection of serious crime, or

(d) action must be taken quickly, for example, in the detection or control of outbreaks of some communicable diseases, and there is insufficient time to contact the patient.

39   You should inform the patient that a disclosure will be made in the public interest, even if you have not sought consent, unless to do so is impracticable, would put you or others at risk of serious harm, or would prejudice the purpose of the disclosure. You must document in the patient's record your reasons for disclosing information without consent and any steps you have taken to seek the patient's consent, to inform them about the disclosure, or your reasons for not doing so.

Research and other secondary uses

40   Research, epidemiology, public health surveillance, health service planning, and education and training are among the important secondary uses made of patient information. Each of these uses can serve important public interests.[14]

41   For many secondary uses, it will be sufficient and practicable to disclose only anonymised or coded information. When identifiable information is needed, or it is not practicable to remove identifiable information, it will often be perfectly practicable to get patients' express consent.

42   You may disclose identifiable information without consent if it is required by law, if it is approved under section 251 of the *NHS Act 2006*,[15] or if it can be justified in the public interest and it is either:

(a)   necessary to use identifiable information, or

(b)   not practicable to anonymise or code the information

and, in either case, not practicable[16] to seek consent (or efforts to seek consent have been unsuccessful).[17]

43   In considering whether it is practicable to seek consent you must take account of:

(a)   the age of records and the likely traceability of patients

(b)   the number of records, and

(c)   the possibility of introducing bias because of a low response rate or because particular groups of patients refuse, or do not respond to, requests to use their information.

44 When considering whether the public interest in disclosures for secondary uses outweighs patients' and the public interest in keeping the information confidential, you must consider:

(a) the nature of the information to be disclosed

(b) what use will be made of the information

(c) how many people will have access to the information

(d) the confidentiality and security arrangements in place to protect the information from further disclosure

(e) the advice of a Caldicott Guardian or similar expert adviser, who is not directly connected with the use for which disclosure is being considered, and

(f) the potential for distress or harm to patients.

45 When considering applications for support under section 251 of the *NHS Act 2006* in England and Wales, the National Information Governance Board considers:

(a) the feasibility of doing the research or other activity with patients' consent or by using anonymised or coded information, and

(b) whether the use of identifiable information would benefit patients or the public sufficiently to outweigh patients' right to privacy.[18]

46 The Privacy Advisory Committee in Northern Ireland can advise on some of the same considerations; but it has no statutory powers and so cannot give lawful authority to disclosures of identifiable information without consent. In the event of a complaint or challenge, its advice on best practice might play an important part in any assessment of the propriety of a disclosure.

47   The Privacy Advisory Committee in Scotland performs a different role, and doctors there should seek the advice of Caldicott Guardians, defence organisations or professional bodies if they are unsure about whether disclosures of identifiable information for secondary uses can be justified in the public interest.

48   It might not be practicable for the healthcare team, or those who usually support them, to anonymise or code information or to seek patients' express consent:

(a) for the disclosure of identifiable information for important secondary uses, or

(b) so that suitable patients can be recruited to clinical trials or other approved research projects.

49   If that is the case:

(a) identifiable information may be sent to a 'safe haven', where they exist and have the capabilities and are otherwise suitable to process the information (including anonymising or coding it) and to manage the disclosure of information for secondary uses or, if that is not practicable[19]

(b) the task of anonymising or coding the information or seeking patients' consent to disclosure can be delegated[20] to someone incorporated into the healthcare team on a temporary basis and bound by legal and contractual obligations of confidentiality.

50　You should only disclose identifiable information for research if that research is approved by a Research Ethics Committee. You should alert Research Ethics Committees to disclosures of identifiable information without consent when applying for approval for research projects.[21]

Disclosures to protect the patient

51　It may be appropriate to encourage patients to consent to disclosures you consider necessary for their protection, and to warn them of the risks of refusing to consent; but you should usually abide by a competent adult patient's refusal to consent to disclosure, even if their decision leaves them, but nobody else, at risk of serious harm.[22] You should do your best to provide patients with the information and support they need to make decisions in their own interests, for example, by arranging contact with agencies that support victims of domestic violence.

52　Disclosure without consent may be justified if it is not practicable to seek a patient's consent. See paragraph 38 for examples, and paragraph 63 for guidance on disclosures to protect a patient who lacks capacity to consent.

Disclosures to protect others

53　Disclosure of personal information about a patient without consent may be justified in the public interest if failure to disclose may expose others to a risk of death or serious harm. You should still seek the patient's consent to disclosure if practicable and consider any reasons given for refusal.

54   Such a situation might arise, for example, when a disclosure would be likely to assist in the prevention, detection or prosecution of serious crime,[23] especially crimes against the person. When victims of violence refuse police assistance, disclosure may still be justified if others remain at risk, for example, from someone who is prepared to use weapons, or from domestic violence when children or others may be at risk.

55   If a patient's refusal to consent to disclosure leaves others exposed to a risk so serious that it outweighs the patient's and the public interest in maintaining confidentiality, or if it is not practicable or safe to seek the patient's consent, you should disclose information promptly to an appropriate person or authority. You should inform the patient before disclosing the information, if practicable and safe, even if you intend to disclose without their consent.

56   You should participate in procedures set up to protect the public from violent and sex offenders. You should co-operate with requests for relevant information about patients who may pose a risk of serious harm to others.[24]

Disclosures about patients who lack capacity to consent

57   There is advice on assessing a patient's mental capacity in our guidance
      Consent: patients and doctors making decisions together and in the *Adults
      with Incapacity (Scotland) Act 2000* and *Mental Capacity Act 2005* codes
      of practice. There is no specific mental capacity legislation for Northern
      Ireland.

58   For advice in relation to children and young people, see our guidance
      0-18 years: guidance for all doctors.

59   When making decisions about whether to disclose information about a
      patient who lacks capacity, you must:

      (a) make the care of the patient your first concern

      (b) respect the patient's dignity and privacy, and

      (c) support and encourage the patient to be involved, as far as they want
          and are able, in decisions about disclosure of their personal information.

60   You must also consider:

      (a) whether the patient's lack of capacity is permanent or temporary and,
          if temporary, whether the decision to disclose could reasonably wait
          until they regain capacity

      (b) any evidence of the patient's previously expressed preferences

      (c) the views of anyone the patient asks you to consult, or who has legal
          authority to make a decision on their behalf, or has been appointed to
          represent them

(d) the views of people close to the patient on the patient's preferences, feelings, beliefs and values, and whether they consider the proposed disclosure to be in the patient's best interests, and

(e) what you and the rest of the healthcare team know about the patient's wishes, feelings, beliefs and values.

61   If a patient who lacks capacity asks you not to disclose personal information about their condition or treatment, you should try to persuade them to allow an appropriate person to be involved in the consultation.[25] If they refuse, and you are convinced that it is essential in their best interests, you may disclose relevant information to an appropriate person or authority. In such a case you should tell the patient before disclosing the information and, if appropriate, seek and carefully consider the views of an advocate or carer. You should document in the patient's record your discussions and the reasons for deciding to disclose the information.

62   You may need to share personal information with a patient's relatives, friends or carers to enable you to assess the patient's best interests. But that does not mean they have a general right of access to the patient's records or to have irrelevant information about, for example, the patient's past healthcare. You should also share relevant personal information with anyone who is authorised to make decisions on behalf of, or who is appointed to support and represent, a mentally incapacitated patient.[26]

Disclosures when a patient may be a victim of neglect or abuse

63   If you believe that a patient may be a victim of neglect or physical, sexual or emotional abuse, and that they lack capacity to consent to disclosure, you must give information promptly to an appropriate responsible person or authority, if you believe that the disclosure is in the patient's best interests or necessary to protect others from a risk of serious harm. If, for any reason, you believe that disclosure of information is not in the best interests of a neglected or abused patient, you should discuss the issues with an experienced colleague. If you decide not to disclose information, you should document in the patient's record your discussions and the reasons for deciding not to disclose. You should be prepared to justify your decision.

Sharing information with a patient's partner, carers, relatives or friends

64   You should establish with the patient what information they want you to share, who with, and in what circumstances. This will be particularly important if the patient has fluctuating or diminished capacity or is likely to lose capacity, even temporarily. Early discussions of this nature can help to avoid disclosures that patients would object to. They can also help to avoid misunderstandings with, or causing offence to, anyone the patient would want information to be shared with.

65   If a patient lacks capacity, you should share relevant information in accordance with the advice in paragraphs 57 to 63. Unless they indicate otherwise, it is reasonable to assume that patients would want those closest to them to be kept informed of their general condition and prognosis.

66   If anyone close to the patient wants to discuss their concerns about the patient's health, you should make it clear to them that, while it is not a breach of confidentiality to listen to their concerns, you cannot guarantee that you will not tell the patient about the conversation. You might need to share with a patient information you have received from others, for example, if it has influenced your assessment and treatment of the patient.[27] You should not refuse to listen to a patient's partner, carers or others on the basis of confidentiality. Their views or the information they provide might be helpful in your care of the patient. You will, though, need to consider whether your patient would consider you listening to the concerns of others about your patient's health or care to be a breach of trust, particularly if they have asked you not to listen to particular people.[28]

Genetic and other shared information

67   Genetic and some other information about your patient might at the same time also be information about others the patient shares genetic or other links with. The diagnosis of an illness in the patient might, for example, point to the certainty or likelihood of the same illness in a blood relative.

68   Most patients will readily share information about their own health with their children and other relatives, particularly if they are advised that it might help those relatives to:

(a) get prophylaxis or other preventative treatments or interventions

(b) make use of increased surveillance or other investigations, or

(c) prepare for potential health problems.[29]

69   However, a patient might refuse to consent to the disclosure of information that would benefit others, for example, where family relationships have broken down, or if their natural children have been adopted. In these circumstances, disclosure might still be justified in the public interest (see paragraphs 36 to 56). If a patient refuses consent to disclosure, you will need to balance your duty to make the care of your patient your first concern against your duty to help protect the other person from serious harm. If practicable, you should not disclose the patient's identity in contacting and advising others of the risks they face.

Disclosure after a patient's death

70 Your duty of confidentiality continues after a patient has died.[30] Whether and what personal information may be disclosed after a patient's death will depend on the circumstances. If the patient had asked for information to remain confidential, you should usually respect their wishes. If you are unaware of any instructions from the patient, when you are considering requests for information you should take into account:

(a) whether the disclosure of information is likely to cause distress to, or be of benefit to, the patient's partner or family[31]

(b) whether the disclosure will also disclose information about the patient's family or anyone else

(c) whether the information is already public knowledge or can be anonymised or coded, and

(d) the purpose of the disclosure.

71 There are circumstances in which you should disclose relevant information about a patient who has died, for example:

(a) to help a coroner, procurator fiscal or other similar officer with an inquest or fatal accident inquiry[32]

(b) when disclosure is required by law, is authorised under section 251 of the *NHS Act 2006*, or is justified in the public interest, such as for education or research

(c) for National Confidential Inquiries or for local clinical audit

(d) on death certificates, which you must complete honestly and fully

(e) for public health surveillance, in which case the information should be anonymised or coded, unless that would defeat the purpose

(f) when a parent asks for information about the circumstances and causes of a child's death

(g) when a partner, close relative or friend asks for information about the circumstances of an adult's death, and you have no reason to believe that the patient would have objected to such a disclosure, and

(h) when a person has a right of access to records under the *Access to Health Records Act 1990* or *Access to Health Records (Northern Ireland) Order 1993.*[33]

72   Archived records relating to deceased patients remain subject to a duty of confidentiality, although the potential for disclosing information about, or causing distress to, surviving relatives or damaging the public's trust will diminish over time.[34]

Glossary

This glossary defines the terms used in this document. These definitions have no wider or legal significance.

Information

Personal information   Information about people which doctors learn in a professional capacity and from which individuals can be identified.

Anonymised information   Information from which individuals cannot reasonably be identified. Names, addresses, full postcodes or identification numbers, alone or together or in conjunction with any other information held by or available to the recipient, can be used to identify patients.

Coded information   Also known as pseudonymised information. Information from which individuals cannot be identified by the recipient, but which enables information about different patients to be distinguished or to link information about the same patients over time (for example, to identify drug side effects). A 'key' might be retained by the person or service which coded the information so that it can be reconnected with the patient. (See *Anonymised information* above.)

Identifiable information   Information from which a patient can be identified. Their name, address and full postcode will identify a patient; combinations of information may also do so, even if their name and address are not included. Information consisting of small numbers and rare conditions might also lead to the identification of an individual. Compare with *Anonymised* and *Coded information*.

Consent

Consent Agreement to an action based on knowledge of what the action involves and its likely consequences.

Express consent Consent which is expressed orally or in writing. Also known as explicit consent.

Implied consent Consent that can be inferred if the patient has been informed that information is to be disclosed, the purpose and extent of the disclosure, and that they have a right to object, but have not objected.

Other terms

Clinical audit Evaluation of clinical performance against standards or through comparative analysis, to inform the management of services.

Disclosure The provision or passing of information about a patient to anyone other than the patient, regardless of the purpose. Sharing information within healthcare teams is a form of disclosure, as is providing personal information about a patient to the police.

Healthcare team The healthcare team comprises the people providing clinical services for a patient, and the administrative and other staff who support the provision of their care. See paragraph 25 and Endnote 9 for more examples of who might form part of the healthcare team.

| Public interest | The interests of the community as a whole, or a group within the community or individuals. Paragraphs 36 and 37 give an explanation of the balancing exercise required to decide if disclosure might be justified in the public interest. |

Legal annex

1   Various bodies regulating healthcare providers and professionals have statutory powers to require the disclosure of information, including personal information about patients. The following represents only a selection of these bodies, a summary of their most relevant powers, and reference to codes they publish about how they use their powers.

2   There are a large number of other Acts that provide for some form of access to information, which may include personal information about patients, for purposes as diverse as the prevention of terrorism and the investigation of road or rail accidents.

3   If you are unsure about the legal basis for a request for information, you should ask for clarification from the person making the request and, if necessary, seek independent legal advice.

Regulation of healthcare providers and professionals

4   The **Care Quality Commission** has powers of inspection, entry and to require documents and information under the *Health and Social Care Act 2008*. Sections 76 to 79 govern the Commission's use and disclosure of confidential personal information. Section 80 requires it to consult on and publish a code of practice on how it obtains, handles, uses and discloses confidential personal information.

5   **Healthcare Inspectorate Wales** has powers under the *Health and Social Care (Community Health and Standards) Act 2003* to access patients' personal information.

6   The **Scottish Care Commission** has similar powers in relation to registered independent healthcare providers under section 25 of the *Regulation of Care (Scotland) Act 2001*.

7   The **Regulation and Quality Improvement Authority** has powers under sections 41 and 42 of the *Health and Personal Social Services (Quality, Improvement and Regulation) (Northern Ireland) Order 2003* to enter establishments and agencies and Health and Social Services bodies or providers' premises and inspect and take copies of records, subject to the protection of confidential information provided for in section 43.

8   The **NHS Counter Fraud Service** has powers under the *NHS Act 2006* and *NHS (Wales) Act 2006* to require the production of documents to prevent, detect and prosecute fraud in the NHS. The Department of Health (England) and Welsh Assembly Government have published codes of practice for the use of these powers.

9   Section 35A of the *Medical Act 1983* gives the **GMC** power to require disclosure of information and documentation relevant to the discharge of our fitness to practise functions, provided such disclosure is not prohibited by other legislation.

10   The **Parliamentary and Health Service Ombudsman, Northern Ireland Ombudsman, Public Service Ombudsman for Wales** and the **Scottish Public Services Ombudsman** have statutory powers similar to the High Court or Court of Session to require the production of documents and the attendance and examination of witnesses for the purposes of investigations about the health bodies that fall within their remits.

Court orders

11   The courts, both civil and criminal, have powers to order disclosure of information in various circumstances. The basis on which disclosure is being ordered should be explained to you; and the patient whose personal information is sought should be told about the order, unless that is not practicable or would undermine the purpose for which disclosure is sought.

Endnotes

1   Caldicott Guardians are senior people in NHS, local authority social care, and partner organisations, who are responsible for protecting the confidentiality of patient information and enabling appropriate information sharing.

2   Doctors working in a managed environment will do this largely by understanding and following corporate information governance and confidentiality policies.

3   The *Data Protection Act 1998* provides for exceptions in some circumstances and allows charges to be made. You can find out more about this in guidance from the Information Commissioner's Office and the UK health departments.

4   The *NHS Code of Practice: Records Management* (Department of Health, 2006), *Records Management: NHS Code of Practice (Scotland)* (Scottish Government, 2008), *Welsh Health Circular (2000) 71: For The Record* (National Assembly for Wales) and *Good Management, Good Records* (Department of Health, Social Services and Public Safety, 2005) all include schedules of minimum retention periods for different types of records. You should also consider any legal requirement of specialty-specific guidance that affects the period for which you should keep records. You should not keep records for longer than necessary.

5   You should follow the technical guidance of the Information Commissioner's Office. The ISO 27001 Security Management Standard and the Code of Practice for Information Security Management in ISO 27002 give more detailed guidance, as does the Department of Health's technical guidance for NHS organisations. NHS Connecting for Health publishes an Information Governance Toolkit for NHS organisations. It aims to bring together, in a single framework, all the requirements, standards and best practice on handling personal information, allowing implementation of Department of Health guidance and compliance with the law.

6   Different diseases are notifiable in different UK countries and the reporting arrangements differ. You can get advice from the Health Protection Agency in England and Wales, Communicable Disease Surveillance Centre in Northern Ireland and Health Protection Scotland.

7   See the legal annex (page 33) for more information about the statutory powers of bodies regulating the provision of healthcare and healthcare professionals to require disclosure of information, and about other legal duties to disclose.

8   You may disclose information to your own legal adviser in order to take their advice.

9   Others who might form part of the healthcare team, but with whom patients might not expect information to be shared, include prescribing advisers who review patients' medicine needs to improve safety, efficacy and efficiency in doctors' prescribing.

10   See *Good Medical Practice* (GMC, 2006), paragraphs 14 and 41.

11   See the supplementary guidance on *Disclosing records for financial and administrative purposes* and *Disclosing information for insurance, employment and similar purposes*. Disclosure necessary to respond to matters raised on a patient's behalf by a Member of Parliament may be made without seeking the patient's express consent; you should still check with the patient if you think they would not reasonably expect the information to be disclosed. See the Information Commissioner's technical guidance note on the *Data Protection (Processing of Sensitive Personal Data) (Elected Representatives) Order 2002*.

12   If any of the exceptions apply, you should still disclose as much of the report as you can. The Department for Work and Pensions publishes advice about reports for benefits purposes.
     See **www.dwp.gov.uk/healthcare-professional/guidance**

13   Section 251 of the *NHS Act 2006* re-enacts section 60 of the *Health and Social Care Act 2001*. Approval under section 251 of the *NHS Act 2006* allows for disclosure despite the common law requirement to obtain consent, but would not usually authorise disclosure to which a patient had objected; disclosure might still be justified in the public interest. See also the guidance in paragraphs 46 and 47 on the roles of the privacy advisory committees in Scotland and Northern Ireland.

14   See the supplementary guidance on *Disclosing records for financial and administrative purposes*, such as QOF reviews, and *Disclosing information for education and training purposes*. The Medical Research Council publishes a toolkit of practical advice on the legal and good practice requirements of using personal information in research.
     See **www.dt-toolkit.ac.uk/home.cfm**

15   Section 251 of the *NHS Act 2006* applies only to England and Wales, where doctors should seek and abide by the independent advice of the Ethics and Confidentiality Committee of the National Information Governance Board.

16   You should consider whether the work needed to anonymise or code the information or to seek patients' consent is reasonably practicable in all the circumstances. Only if unreasonable effort is required should you go on to consider whether disclosure of identifiable information is justified in the public interest.

17   If it is not practicable to anonymise or code the information or to seek or obtain patients' consent without unreasonable effort, and the likelihood of distress or harm to patients is negligible, disclosure for an important secondary purpose may be proportionate. You should respect patients' objections to disclosure.

18   Disclosures covered by a regulation are not in breach of the common law duty of confidentiality.

19   The NHS Information Centre is working towards the establishment of the structures and guidance (and seeking approval under section 251 of the *NHS Act 2006*) for safe havens in England. The Information Services Division manages identifiable information about patients for many secondary uses in Scotland.

20   Delegation involves asking a colleague to anonymise or code the information or seek patients' consent. Although you will not be accountable for the actions of those you delegate to, you will still be accountable for your decision to delegate. You must be satisfied that the person you delegate to is trained and understands their responsibilities and the consequences of breaching confidentiality. See paragraphs 12 to 16 on protecting information and the management of records.

21   You might seek Research Ethics Committees' advice on the ethics of disclosing and using identifiable information for research purposes. However, they cannot authorise unconsented disclosure or determine if disclosure is justified in the public interest.

22   The *Adult Support and Protection (Scotland) Act 2007* requires health boards in Scotland to report to local authorities if they know or believe that an adult is at risk of harm (but not necessarily incapacitated) and that action needs to be taken to protect them. The Act also requires certain public bodies and office-holders to co-operate with local authorities making inquiries about adults at risk and includes powers to examine health records for related purposes.

23   There is no agreed definition of 'serious crime'. *Confidentiality: NHS Code of Practice* (Department of Health, 2003) gives some examples of serious crime (including murder, manslaughter, rape and child abuse; serious harm to the security of the state and public order and 'crimes that involve substantial financial gain or loss' are mentioned in the same category). It also gives examples of crimes that are not usually serious enough to warrant disclosure without consent (including theft, fraud, and damage to property where loss or damage is less substantial).

24   You should consider the assessment of risk posed by patients made by other professionals and by groups established for that purpose, but you must make your own assessment and decision as to whether disclosure is justified. Your assessment of risk is a matter of professional judgement in which an offender's past behaviour will be a factor. The Royal College of Psychiatrists publishes guidance for psychiatrists about sharing information in the context of public protection, including participation in Multi-Agency Public Protection Arrangements (MAPPA) and panels.

25   In some cases disclosure will be required or necessary, for example, under the provisions of mental health and mental capacity legislation.

26   This might be a welfare attorney, a court-appointed deputy or guardian or an Independent Mental Capacity Advocate. See the *Adults with Incapacity (Scotland) Act 2000* and *Mental Capacity Act 2005* and their respective codes of practice. There is no specific mental capacity legislation for Northern Ireland, where the common law duty to act in incapacitated patients' best interests endures. Independent Mental Health Advocates should also be provided with the information listed in section 130B of the *Mental Health Act 1983*.

27   Section 7 of the *Data Protection Act 1998* gives patients the right to have access to their personal information; but there are some exceptions. For example, you do not have to supply a patient with information about another person or that identifies another person as the source of the information, unless that other person consents or it is reasonable in the circumstances to supply the information without their consent. See the Information Commissioner's technical guidance note on *Dealing with subject access requests involving other people's information*.

28   The Princess Royal Trust for Carers publishes information on good practice for primary care, mental health and hospital-based professionals, highlighting carers' need for information to perform their roles.

29   For more information see *Consent and confidentiality in genetic practice: Guidance on genetic testing and sharing of genetic information – A report of the Joint Committee on Medical Genetics* (Royal College of Physicians, 2006).

30   There is an obvious ethical obligation. There may also be a legal obligation: see *Lewis v Secretary of State for Health* [2008] EWHC 2196. Section 38 of the *Freedom of Information (Scotland) Act 2002* includes a deceased person's medical records within the definition of personal information, which is exempt from the general entitlement to information.

31   The permission of a surviving relative or next of kin is not required for, and does not authorise, disclosure of confidential information, although the views of those who were close to the patient may help you decide if disclosure is appropriate.

32   See paragraph 69 of *Good Medical Practice* (GMC, 2006).

33   Namely, a deceased patient's personal representative and any person who may have a claim arising out of a patient's death. This is not a general right, and access should be limited to information of relevance to the claim. Access should be limited or refused if there is evidence that the patient would have expected that the information would not be disclosed to the applicant, if disclosure is likely to cause serious harm to anyone else, or if it would also disclose information about a third party (other than a healthcare professional involved in the deceased person's care) who does not consent. Access must be refused to records that contain a note, made at the patient's request, that they did not wish access to be given on an application under the *Access to Health Records Act 1990*.

34   You should contact your organisation's approved place of deposit or The National Archives, the Public Record Office of Northern Ireland or the National Archives of Scotland for further advice about storage of, and access to, archives of records of ongoing research or historical value. Health records of deceased patients are exempt from the *Freedom of Information (Scotland) Act 2002*.

Index

serious harm 51–56, 63
service planning, disclosure for 7
sex offenders 56
solicitors 22
staff, legal duty of confidentiality 28

T
terrorism legal annex 2
third parties
    disclosure to 22
    express consent for disclosure to 34
    to protect 53–56
training (and education) 4f, 40,
    endnote 14
trust 6, 66

V
victims
    disclosure to protect patients at risk
        of neglect or abuse 63
    domestic violence 51, 54
violence
    domestic 51, 54
    if victim refuses police help 54
violent offenders 56

W
weapons, disclosure in public interest
    54
*Welsh Health Circular (2000) 71: For the
    Record* endnote 4

Y
young people, capacity and disclosure
    58

Notes

Confidentiality